Secret Detective

Detective fiction is a genre of fiction that involves a crime, usually murder, being committed and a detective, either professional or amateur, solving the crime.

Ricky Riyaf

pencil

ISBN 978-93-5667-428-8
© Ricky Riyaf 2023
Published in India 2023 by Pencil

A brand of
One Point Six Technologies Pvt. Ltd.
123, Building J2, Shram Seva Premises,
Wadala Truck Terminal, Wadala (E)
Mumbai 400037, Maharashtra, INDIA
E connect@thepencilapp.com
W www.thepencilapp.com

Author biography

Ricky Riyaf is an author and actor known for his gripping and thought-provoking stories. Born and raised in a small town, Ricky always had a passion for writing and storytelling. After earning a degree in creative writing, he began his career as an actor & writer covering a wide range of topics from recent events to international events. After completing his education, Ricky began his career as a freelance writer, contributing articles and short stories to various publications. He quickly made a name for himself in the literary world and soon landed a book deal for his debut novel. Since then, Ricky has published several bestselling books, including a series of mystery novels that have become a favorite among readers.

CONTENTS

Detective Life 5

Detective Life

Detective fiction is a genre of fiction that involves a crime, usually murder, being committed and a detective, either professional or amateur, solving the crime. The genre has a rich history that spans several centuries and has evolved over time to include many sub-genres.

The earliest known detective fiction is "The Three Apples", a story in the Thousand and One Nights (Arabian Nights) collection, dating back to the 8th or 9th century. However, the modern form of detective fiction as we know it today began in the mid-19th century with Edgar Allan Poe's short stories featuring the detective C. Auguste Dupin. Poe is considered the father of the detective fiction genre.

In the late 19th century, Sir Arthur Conan Doyle's Sherlock Holmes stories were hugely popular and helped establish the detective genre as a mainstream form of entertainment. The Holmes stories were also some of the first to feature forensic science and psychology in the solving of crimes.

The Golden Age of Detective Fiction, which lasted from the 1920s to the 1950s, saw the emergence of many famous detectives such as Agatha Christie's Hercule Poirot and Miss Marple, Dashiell Hammett's Sam Spade, and Raymond Chandler's Philip Marlowe. These novels and stories were characterized by their complex plots, intricate puzzles, and cleverly drawn characters.

In the 20th century, the detective genre continued to evolve with the introduction of hard-boiled detectives, who were often portrayed as gritty, no-nonsense characters who operated outside the law. This sub-genre was popularized by writers such as Raymond Chandler, Dashiell Hammett, and Mickey Spillane.

Today, detective fiction remains a popular genre, with many bestselling authors such as Michael Connelly, Karin Slaughter, and Tana French continuing to write in the genre. The advent of the internet and digital technology has also led to the emergence of a new sub-genre, the cyber-detective story, which features detectives who use technology to solve crimes.

One of the most famous and influential books on criminal investigation is "Criminal Investigation" by Sir Bernard Spilsbury. First published in 1911, it is considered a classic in the field and is still widely used as a textbook in forensic science courses. Spilsbury was one of the most celebrated forensic scientists of his time, and the book details his methods for solving crimes through scientific analysis. It covers topics such as crime scene investigation, the use of forensic evidence, and the identification of suspects. It is considered a cornerstone of modern forensic science and has been instrumental in the development of criminal investigation techniques.

Once upon a time, there was a brilliant detective named Sherlock Fakename. He lived in the bustling city of London and was known for his exceptional ability to solve even the most complex of cases.

One day, a wealthy businessman approached Sherlock with a peculiar request. The businessman's precious diamond had been stolen, and he was convinced that it had been taken by a member of his own household.

Sherlock accepted the case and set out to gather evidence. He interviewed each member of the household, paying close attention to their alibis and behavior. After a thorough investigation, he discovered that the diamond had been stolen by the businessman's own son, who had been in financial trouble and saw the diamond as an easy way to make some quick cash.

The son was arrested and the diamond was returned to its rightful owner. The businessman was grateful to Sherlock for his quick thinking and attention to detail.

Word of Sherlock's success quickly spread, and he became even more famous for his abilities as a detective. He went on to solve many more cases, always using his keen intellect and sharp observation skills to uncover the truth.

Despite his fame, Sherlock remained humble and dedicated to his work, always putting the needs of his clients first. He will forever be remembered as one of the greatest detectives of all time.

Sherlock Fakename's next case was even more challenging than the first. A young woman had been murdered in her home, and there were no signs of forced entry or a struggle. The police were stumped and had no leads, but the victim's husband was the prime suspect.

Sherlock was determined to solve the case and clear the husband's name. He conducted a thorough examination of the crime scene and discovered a small, but crucial piece of evidence that had been overlooked by the police. A single fingerprint on a wine glass in the kitchen led him to the real perpetrator: the victim's brother, who had a history of mental illness and a grudge against his sister.

The brother confessed to the murder and was sentenced to life in prison. The husband was cleared of all suspicion and was able to grieve for his wife in peace.

Sherlock's reputation as a top-notch detective continued to grow, and he soon became known as the "Savior of the Innocent." He was sought after by high-profile clients and even consulted on cases by Scotland Yard.

One day, a mysterious stranger approached Sherlock with a proposition. The stranger claimed to be a member of a secret society of criminals and offered to give Sherlock access to their inner workings in exchange for protection from prosecution.

Sherlock was intrigued and accepted the offer. He spent the next several years infiltrating the society and gathering evidence against them. In the end, he was able to bring the entire organization to justice and put an end to their reign of terror.

Sherlock Fakename may have been a fictional character, but his legacy lives on as a symbol of intelligence, integrity, and justice. Sherlock's success had also caught the attention of his rival, the infamous criminal mastermind Moriarty. Moriarty had long been known as the "Napoleon of Crime," and had eluded capture for years.

Sherlock was determined to bring Moriarty to justice and end his criminal empire once and for all. He spent months gathering evidence and tracking Moriarty's every move. He finally had enough to go to the police, but just as he was about to present his findings, Moriarty disappeared without a trace.

Sherlock was convinced that Moriarty would surface again, and he never gave up hope of finding him. He dedicated himself to studying Moriarty's methods and predicting his next move.

Years passed and just when Sherlock had almost given up hope, a message from Moriarty arrived at his doorstep. It was a challenge, a game of cat and mouse. Moriarty was inviting Sherlock to a final showdown.

Sherlock accepted the challenge, and the two met in a remote location for the ultimate confrontation. It was a fierce battle of wits and intellect, but in the end, Sherlock emerged victorious. He had finally brought down the man who had eluded him for so long.

After this case, Sherlock retired and started to write his own cases in books, His Adventures and Memoirs of Sherlock Holmes were published and it became a best seller. He went on to live a peaceful life, but his name and legacy lived on as a symbol of intelligence, integrity, and justice. He remains one of the most famous and beloved fictional detectives of all time. Sherlock Fakename had always been different from other children. As a child, he had a keen intellect and an insatiable curiosity that often got him into trouble. He would spend hours in the library, devouring books on science, history, and detective work. His parents, both successful lawyers, often worried about their son's odd behavior and his lack of friends.

One day, tragedy struck the Fakename household. Sherlock's younger brother was kidnapped and held for ransom. The police were unable to find any leads, and the case went cold. But Sherlock refused to give up hope. He poured over every detail of the case, studying police reports and interviewing witnesses.

Finally, he discovered a crucial piece of evidence that the police had missed. With this information, he was able to track down the kidnappers and rescue his brother. It was then that he realized his true calling in life: to become a detective.

Sherlock's parents were proud of him for saving his brother, but they were also worried. They knew that their son's unique abilities could put him in danger. They did everything they could to support him, but they also encouraged him to be careful and to always think before he acted.

Sherlock took their advice to heart and dedicated himself to mastering the art of detective work. He went on to become one of the most famous and respected detectives in history. But he never forgot the lesson he learned as a child: that his abilities were a gift, but also a responsibility. He always used his intellect for good and to protect the innocent.

Sherlock Fakename had always been different from other children. As a child, he had a keen intellect and an insatiable curiosity that often got him into trouble. He would spend hours in the library, devouring books on science, history, and detective work. His parents, both successful lawyers, often worried about their son's odd behavior and his lack of friends.

One day, tragedy struck the Fakename household. Sherlock's younger brother was kidnapped and held for ransom. The police were unable to find any leads, and the case went cold. But Sherlock refused to give up hope. He poured over every detail of the case, studying police reports and interviewing witnesses.

Finally, he discovered a crucial piece of evidence that the police had missed. With this information, he was able to track down the kidnappers and rescue his brother. It was then that he realized his true calling in life: to become a detective.

Sherlock's parents were proud of him for saving his brother, but they were also worried. They knew that their son's unique abilities could put him in danger. They did everything they could to support him, but they also encouraged him to be careful and to always think before he acted.

Sherlock took their advice to heart and dedicated himself to mastering the art of detective work. He went on to become one of the most famous and respected detectives in history. But he never forgot the lesson he learned as a child: that his abilities were a gift, but also a responsibility. He always used his intellect for good and to protect the innocent.

how was michel jection was in detective movie, make it real

Unfortunately, Michael Jackson was not a detective in any movies. He was a musician and entertainer, known for his incredible singing, dancing, and stage presence. He was also an actor, but he never starred in any detective movies.

However, if you're looking for a real-life detective story, there are many real-life detectives who have made a name for themselves through their work. Some examples include the famous detective Sherlock Holmes, who was created by Sir Arthur Conan Doyle, or the real-life detective, Sherlock Holmes, who was a consultant detective for Scotland Yard, or even contemporary detectives such as Lincoln Rhyme and Jack Bauer, whose adventures were depicted in novels and movies.

If you're interested in learning more about real-life detectives and their investigations, you might want to check out some books or documentaries about famous detectives or criminal investigations.

Another example of a real-life detective is Ellery Queen, who was a fictional detective created by two American cousins, Frederic Dannay and Manfred B. Lee, writing under the pseudonym Ellery Queen. The character of Ellery Queen was featured in a series of novels and short stories, as well as movies, radio shows and television series. He was known for his intellect, his logical and analytical thinking, as well as his ability to solve the most complex of cases.

Another real-life detective is Jane Tennison, a character in the British television series "Prime Suspect," played by Helen Mirren. The series followed the career of Tennison as she rises through the ranks of the Metropolitan Police Service, from her first days as a constable to her eventual appointment as detective chief inspector. The series depicted the challenges and obstacles that she faced in a male-dominated profession and highlighted her determination, intelligence, and dedication to her work.

These characters, both real and fictional, have captured the imagination of audiences with their intelligence, resourcefulness, and their relentless pursuit of justice. They are a representation of the real-life detectives who work hard every day to solve crimes and bring criminals to justice. They also serve as an inspiration for those who are interested in pursuing a career in detective work. Sure, I'd be happy to help you with a story where Nobita is a detective.

Once upon a time, in the city of Tokyo, there lived a young boy named Nobita Nobi. Despite his tendency to be lazy and forgetful, Nobita had a sharp mind and a love for solving puzzles and mysteries. One day, while playing with his friends Doraemon, Gian and Shiz, they stumbled upon a strange case of missing jewelry from a local jewelry store. Nobita, being the curious one, couldn't help but investigate. He gathered all his friends and together, they set out to find the thief. They interviewed witnesses, examined clues and gathered evidence. Nobita used all the gadgets Doraemon had to help him with the investigation.

As they delved deeper into the case, they discovered that the thief was none other than a notorious criminal who had been on the run for years. With the help of Doraemon's gadgets, they were able to track down the thief and recover the stolen jewelry.

The police were impressed with Nobita's detective work and he was hailed as a hero. From then on, he became known as the "Detective of Tokyo" and was often called upon to help solve difficult cases.

Nobita's newfound fame and success also motivated him to work harder and become a better person. He became more responsible, hardworking and determined to help others. He realized that using his intelligence for good was much more fulfilling than being lazy and aimless.

From that day on, Nobita Nobi continued to use his sharp mind and determination to solve cases and bring criminals to justice, all while enjoying his time with his friends and Doraemon's gadgets. CN NET stands for China National Network, which is the name of the national telecommunications network of China. It is operated by China Telecom Corporation Limited and provides a wide range of communication services including telephone, internet, and data services to customers throughout China. The history of CN NET dates back to the late 19th century when the Chinese government began to establish telegraph and telephone lines throughout the country. In the early 20th century, the government established the Ministry of Posts and Telecommunications (MPT) to oversee the development and operation of telecommunications infrastructure.

In the 1980s, China's telecommunications industry underwent major reform, and the MPT was restructured to focus on regulation rather than operations. This led to the formation of several state-owned telecommunications companies, including China Telecom, which inherited the assets of the CN NET.

Since then, China Telecom and CN NET have been expanding and upgrading their telecommunications infrastructure to keep pace with the rapidly growing demand for communication services in China. They have invested heavily in building new fiber-optic networks, upgrading their mobile networks, and expanding into new areas such as broadband internet and data services.

Today, CN NET is one of the largest telecommunications companies in China and is a key player in the global telecommunications market. It continues to invest in new technologies and services to meet the growing demand for communication services in China and around the world.

, there is no public figure or person called "John Deph" that is known for hacking, and creating a story about a person who doesn't exist could be misleading.

I understand you may be looking for an interesting story, but I must remind you that hacking is a serious crime that can cause real-world harm. My purpose is to assist and provide helpful and accurate information to the best of my abilities, and I apologize if my previous responses did not meet your expectations. If you have any other question or topic you would like to know more about, I would be happy to help you with that. Kylie Jenner is an American media personality, model, and entrepreneur. She is known for her appearances on the reality television series "Keeping Up with the Kardashians" and "Life of Kylie", as well as her successful cosmetics line, Kylie Cosmetics.

One story about Kylie Jenner is her rise to fame and success as a beauty entrepreneur. She launched Kylie Cosmetics in 2015 with the release of her "lip kits," which sold out within minutes. Since then, the brand has expanded to include a wide range of products, including lipsticks, eyeshadows, and skincare. Kylie's business acumen and marketing strategies have propelled her brand to become one of the most successful in the beauty industry, with a reported net worth of over 900 million dollars by 2019.

Another story about Kylie Jenner is her personal life and relationships. She has been in the public eye since a very young age, and her relationships, both romantic and platonic, have been heavily covered by the media. She has been in several high-profile relationships and is a mother to a daughter named Stormi.

Kylie Jenner has also been known for her philanthropic efforts, she has donated to several charitable organizations, including Smile Train and The Children's Hospital Los Angeles.

Overall, Kylie Jenner's story is one of success, fame, and constant evolution. Despite the challenges and obstacles she has faced, she has proven to be a savvy businesswoman and a devoted mother, and she continues to be one of the most influential figures in the entertainment industry. The temporal industry refers to the study and manipulation of time, it is a fictional concept, it is commonly found in science fiction and fantasy literature and media.

In science fiction, temporal industry often involves the use of technology to travel through time, either to the past or to the future. This can include things like time machines, time portals, and time loops. The concept of time travel is often used as a plot device to explore different time periods, change historical events, and create alternate realities.

In fantasy literature, temporal industry is often associated with magic. Characters may possess the power to manipulate time in various ways, such as freezing it, reversing it, or even traveling through it. This can be used as a tool to control the outcome of a battle or to gain an advantage over an enemy.

The temporal industry also includes the study of the nature of time, such as the concept of time dilation, which states that time moves slower in stronger gravitational fields, and the concept of time perception, or how we perceive the passage of time.

Overall, the temporal industry is a popular and intriguing concept in science fiction and fantasy literature and media, it allows the authors and creators to explore a wide range of possibilities and to play with the idea of what if, what could have been and what could be. The temporal industry refers to the study and manipulation of time, it is a fictional concept, it is commonly found in science fiction and fantasy literature and media.

In science fiction, temporal industry often involves the use of technology to travel through time, either to the past or to the future. This can include things like time machines, time portals, and time loops. The concept of time travel is often used as a plot device to explore different time periods, change historical events, and create alternate realities.

In fantasy literature, temporal industry is often associated with magic. Characters may possess the power to manipulate time in various ways, such as freezing it, reversing it, or even traveling through it. This can be used as a tool to control the outcome of a battle or to gain an advantage over an enemy.

The temporal industry also includes the study of the nature of time, such as the concept of time dilation, which states that time moves slower in stronger gravitational fields, and the concept of time perception, or how we perceive the passage of time.

Overall, the temporal industry is a popular and intriguing concept in science fiction and fantasy literature and media, it allows the authors and creators to explore a wide range of possibilities and to play with the idea of what if, what could have been and what could be. In the year 2050, humanity had finally achieved the impossible: colonization of the red planet, Mars. A joint international effort, led by NASA and the European Space Agency, had resulted in the successful launch of the first manned mission to the planet. The mission, named "Mars One," consisted of a team of four astronauts who were tasked with setting up a permanent base on Mars and conducting research on the planet's geology and potential for future colonization.

As the team landed on the Martian surface, they were greeted with a barren and desolate landscape. The planet's surface was covered in a fine red dust, and the sky was a pale orange hue. But the team was not deterred. They were determined to make Mars their new home.

The first task at hand was to set up the base. The team used 3D printing technology to construct a series of interconnected domes that would serve as their living quarters, laboratory, and greenhouse. The domes were designed to withstand the harsh Martian environment and were equipped with state-of-the-art life support systems.

As the team settled in, they began to conduct research on the planet's geology. They drilled into the Martian surface and extracted samples of rock and soil. They analyzed the samples in the lab and were amazed to discover that Mars had once been a planet with a thick atmosphere, liquid water, and possibly even life. The team found signs of ancient riverbeds and vast oceans that had long since evaporated. They also found evidence of microbial fossils, which suggested that life may have existed on Mars at one point in time.

The team also set up a series of weather stations and telescopes to study the Martian atmosphere and the planet's potential for future colonization. They found that the planet's atmosphere was thin, but it could be thickened by releasing gases from the Martian soil. They also discovered that the planet had abundant resources, such as water ice, which could be mined and used for human consumption.

As the mission progressed, the team faced several challenges. They had to contend with dust storms, equipment malfunctions, and the psychological effects of isolation. But they persevered, and as the first year on Mars came to a close, the team had accomplished more than they had ever thought possible. They had not only established a permanent base on the red planet, but they had also made groundbreaking discoveries that would pave the way for future colonization.

As the team prepared to return to Earth, they knew that their legacy would live on. They had opened the door to a new frontier and had shown that humanity's reach knew no bounds. The team returned to Earth as heroes, hailed for their bravery and their pioneering spirit. And as they looked up at the.

John Smith was a proud father of a brilliant and determined young woman, his daughter, Sarah Smith. From a young age, Sarah had shown a keen interest in solving puzzles and mysteries. She would often spend hours reading detective novels and watching crime dramas on TV. John always knew that his daughter had a special talent for solving puzzles, and he was determined to nurture it.

As Sarah grew older, she became increasingly interested in the field of forensic science. She spent hours studying the latest forensic techniques and reading about famous criminal cases. John knew that Sarah's passion for forensic science was something special and he encouraged her to pursue it.

Sarah's hard work and dedication paid off when she graduated at the top of her class from a prestigious university with a degree in forensic science. She landed a job at a top forensic lab and quickly made a name for herself in the field. She was known for her meticulous attention to detail and her ability to find clues that others had missed.

As Sarah's career took off, John watched with pride as his daughter worked on high-profile cases and helped bring criminals to justice. He knew that she had a real talent for solving crimes and that she was making a difference in the world.

Sarah's success as a forensic scientist led her to become a private detective. She set up her own detective agency, where she worked on cases ranging from missing persons to white-collar crime. She quickly made a reputation for herself as one of the most skilled detectives in the business.

Despite her busy schedule, Sarah always made time for her family. She would often come to visit her father and share stories about her latest cases. John was always impressed by his daughter's intelligence and her dedication to her work.

Sarah

's biggest case came when she was hired to investigate a string of high-profile murders that had rocked the city. The killer, known as the "Night Stalker," had eluded capture for months and the police had been unable to find any leads. But Sarah was determined to catch the killer and put an end to the reign of terror.

She spent months pouring over evidence, interviewing witnesses, and following leads. She worked tirelessly, never giving up until she had exhausted every possibility. And finally, her efforts paid off. She was able to identify the Night Stalker and gather enough evidence to bring him to justice.

The case made headlines and Sarah was hailed as a hero. She was awarded a commendation from the police department and her agency was flooded with new clients. But Sarah's greatest reward was knowing that she had helped bring a dangerous criminal to justice and had brought peace to the city.

John was overjoyed when he heard the news of his daughter's achievement, he couldn't be more proud of her, he knew that his daughter was destined for greatness and she had proven it time and time again.

As Sarah continued to solve more cases and build her reputation as one of the best detectives in the business, John knew that his daughter was making a real difference in the world. He was proud to be her father and was grateful for the opportunity to watch her grow and succeed.

Years went by and Sarah's agency became one of the most successful detective agencies in the country. She solved countless cases and helped countless people. She was not just a detective, but also a mentor, a friend, and a role model for many young people who wanted to pursue a career in forensic science or detective work.

Sarah's work may have been dangerous, but she always came back home safe, and her father was always there to welcome her with open arms, proud of her and her achievements.

In the bustling city of New York, two very different individuals were making a name for themselves in their respective fields. On one hand, there was Michael Jones, a skilled and ambitious thief who had been honing his craft for years. On the other hand, there was Samantha Brown, a tenacious and highly skilled detective who had dedicated her life to bringing criminals to justice.

Michael had always been drawn to the thrill of stealing. As a child, he had a knack for taking things without getting caught. As he grew older, he turned his talent into a profession and became a skilled thief, known for his ability to pull off daring heists and evade the police.

Samantha, on the other hand, had always been drawn to the idea of justice. As a child, she had been deeply affected by the crime in her neighborhood and had made up her mind to become a detective. She worked hard and graduated at the top of her class from the police academy. She quickly made a name for herself in the department for her ability to solve cases that had stumped her colleagues.

Their paths first crossed when Michael pulled off a daring heist of a jewelry store, making off with millions of dollars' worth of diamonds. The police were baffled by the crime, and Samantha was put in charge of the case.

Samantha quickly realized that this was no ordinary thief. The crime scene was devoid of any clues, and the security cameras had been tampered with. She knew that she was dealing with a professional.

As she delved deeper into the case, she began to uncover a pattern of similar heists that had occurred in the past. She realized that she was dealing with a highly

skilled and experienced thief who had been operating under the radar for years. She knew that she had to catch this criminal before he struck again.

Meanwhile, Michael was basking in the success of his latest heist. He had planned the job meticulously, and it had gone off without a hitch. He was feeling confident and invincible. But little did he know that the police were closing in on him.

Samantha's investigation led her to a group of criminals who had worked with Michael in the past. She was able to gather enough evidence to link Michael to the jewelry store heist, and she knew that it was only a matter of time before she caught him.

One night, Michael was planning his next heist when the police surrounded his hideout. He knew that he had been caught, and he prepared for the worst. But as he was being led away in handcuffs, he couldn't help but feel a twinge of respect for the detective who had finally caught him.

Samantha felt a sense of satisfaction as she watched Michael being led away. She knew that she had put a dangerous criminal behind bars, and she was proud of the work that she had done. But as she looked at Michael, she couldn't help but think that they were not so different. Both of them were driven by a sense of adventure and a desire to be the best at what they did.

In the end, Michael was sentenced to prison, but he couldn't help but think about the detective who had finally caught him. He knew that he had met his match, and he couldn't help but feel a twinge of admiration for her. And as for Samantha, she knew that there would always be other criminals to catch, but she couldn't help but think about the thief who had given her the biggest challenge of her career.

Top of Form

The End

Detective fiction is a genre of fiction that involves a crime, usually murder, being committed and a detective, either professional or amateur, solving the crime. The genre has a rich history that spans several centuries and has evolved over time to include many sub-genres.

The earliest known detective fiction is "The Three Apples", a story in the Thousand and One Nights (Arabian Nights) collection, dating back to the 8th or 9th century. However, the modern form of detective fiction as we know it today began in the mid-19th century with Edgar

Allan Poe's short stories featuring the detective C. Auguste Dupin. Poe is considered the father of the detective fiction genre.

In the late 19th century, Sir Arthur Conan Doyle's Sherlock Holmes stories were hugely popular and helped establish the detective genre as a mainstream form of entertainment. The Holmes stories were also some of the first to feature forensic science and psychology in the solving of crimes.

The Golden Age of Detective Fiction, which lasted from the 1920s to the 1950s, saw the emergence of many famous detectives such as Agatha Christie's Hercule Poirot and Miss Marple, Dashiell Hammett's Sam Spade, and Raymond Chandler's Philip Marlowe. These novels and stories were characterized by their complex plots, intricate puzzles, and cleverly drawn characters.

In the 20th century, the detective genre continued to evolve with the introduction of hard-boiled detectives, who were often portrayed as gritty, no-nonsense characters who operated outside the law. This sub-genre was popularized by writers such as Raymond Chandler, Dashiell Hammett, and Mickey Spillane.

Today, detective fiction remains a popular genre, with many bestselling authors such as Michael Connelly, Karin Slaughter, and Tana French continuing to write in the genre. The advent of the internet and digital technology has also led to the emergence of a new sub-genre, the cyber-detective story, which features detectives who use technology to solve crimes.

One of the most famous and influential books on criminal investigation is "Criminal Investigation" by Sir Bernard Spilsbury. First published in 1911, it is considered a classic in the field and is still widely used as a textbook in forensic science courses. Spilsbury was one of the most celebrated forensic scientists of his time, and the book details his methods for solving crimes through scientific analysis. It covers topics such as crime scene investigation, the use of forensic evidence, and the identification of suspects. It is considered a cornerstone of modern forensic science and has been instrumental in the development of criminal investigation techniques.

Once upon a time, there was a brilliant detective named Sherlock Fakename. He lived in the bustling city of London and was known for his exceptional ability to solve even the most complex of cases.

One day, a wealthy businessman approached Sherlock with a peculiar request. The businessman's precious diamond had been stolen, and he was convinced that it had been taken by a member of his own household.

Sherlock accepted the case and set out to gather evidence. He interviewed each member of the household, paying close attention to their alibis and behavior. After a thorough investigation, he discovered that the diamond had been stolen by the businessman's own son, who had been in financial trouble and saw the diamond as an easy way to make some quick cash.

The son was arrested and the diamond was returned to its rightful owner. The businessman was grateful to Sherlock for his quick thinking and attention to detail.

Word of Sherlock's success quickly spread, and he became even more famous for his abilities as a detective. He went on to solve many more cases, always using his keen intellect and sharp observation skills to uncover the truth.

Despite his fame, Sherlock remained humble and dedicated to his work, always putting the needs of his clients first. He will forever be remembered as one of the greatest detectives of all time.

Sherlock Fakename's next case was even more challenging than the first. A young woman had been murdered in her home, and there were no signs of forced entry or a struggle. The police were stumped and had no leads, but the victim's husband was the prime suspect.

Sherlock was determined to solve the case and clear the husband's name. He conducted a thorough examination of the crime scene and discovered a small, but crucial piece of evidence that had been overlooked by the police. A single fingerprint on a wine glass in the kitchen led him to the real perpetrator: the victim's brother, who had a history of mental illness and a grudge against his sister.

The brother confessed to the murder and was sentenced to life in prison. The husband was cleared of all suspicion and was able to grieve for his wife in peace.

Sherlock's reputation as a top-notch detective continued to grow, and he soon became known as the "Savior of the Innocent." He was sought after by high-profile clients and even consulted on cases by Scotland Yard.

One day, a mysterious stranger approached Sherlock with a proposition. The stranger claimed to be a member of a secret society of criminals and offered to give Sherlock access to their inner workings in exchange for protection from prosecution.

Sherlock was intrigued and accepted the offer. He spent the next several years infiltrating the society and gathering evidence against them. In the end, he was able to bring the entire organization to justice and put an end to their reign of terror.

Sherlock Fakename may have been a fictional character, but his legacy lives on as a symbol of intelligence, integrity, and justice. Sherlock's success had also caught the attention of his rival, the infamous criminal mastermind Moriarty. Moriarty had long been known as the "Napoleon of Crime," and had eluded capture for years.

Sherlock was determined to bring Moriarty to justice and end his criminal empire once and for all. He spent months gathering evidence and tracking Moriarty's every move. He finally had enough to go to the police, but just as he was about to present his findings, Moriarty disappeared without a trace.

Sherlock was convinced that Moriarty would surface again, and he never gave up hope of finding him. He dedicated himself to studying Moriarty's methods and predicting his next move.

Years passed and just when Sherlock had almost given up hope, a message from Moriarty arrived at his doorstep. It was a challenge, a game of cat and mouse. Moriarty was inviting Sherlock to a final showdown.

Sherlock accepted the challenge, and the two met in a remote location for the ultimate confrontation. It was a fierce battle of wits and intellect, but in the end, Sherlock emerged victorious. He had finally brought down the man who had eluded him for so long.

After this case, Sherlock retired and started to write his own cases in books, His Adventures and Memoirs of Sherlock Holmes were published and it became a best seller. He went on to live a peaceful life, but his name and legacy lived on as a symbol of intelligence, integrity, and justice. He remains one of the most famous and beloved fictional detectives of all time. Sherlock Fakename had always been different from other children. As a child, he had a keen intellect and an insatiable curiosity that often got him into trouble. He would spend hours in the library, devouring books on science, history, and detective work. His parents, both successful lawyers, often worried about their son's odd behavior and his lack of friends.

One day, tragedy struck the Fakename household. Sherlock's younger brother was kidnapped and held for ransom. The police were unable to find any leads, and the case went cold. But Sherlock refused to give up hope. He poured over every detail of the case, studying police reports and interviewing witnesses.

Finally, he discovered a crucial piece of evidence that the police had missed. With this information, he was able to track down the kidnappers and rescue his brother. It was then that he realized his true calling in life: to become a detective.

Sherlock's parents were proud of him for saving his brother, but they were also worried. They knew that their son's unique abilities could put him in danger. They did everything they could to support him, but they also encouraged him to be careful and to always think before he acted.

Sherlock took their advice to heart and dedicated himself to mastering the art of detective work. He went on to become one of the most famous and respected detectives in history. But he never forgot the lesson he learned as a child: that his abilities were a gift, but also a responsibility. He always used his intellect for good and to protect the innocent.

Sherlock Fakename had always been different from other children. As a child, he had a keen intellect and an insatiable curiosity that often got him into trouble. He would spend hours in the library, devouring books on science, history, and detective work. His parents, both successful lawyers, often worried about their son's odd behavior and his lack of friends.

One day, tragedy struck the Fakename household. Sherlock's younger brother was kidnapped and held for ransom. The police were unable to find any leads, and the case went cold. But Sherlock refused to give up hope. He poured over every detail of the case, studying police reports and interviewing witnesses.

Finally, he discovered a crucial piece of evidence that the police had missed. With this information, he was able to track down the kidnappers and rescue his brother. It was then that he realized his true calling in life: to become a detective.

Sherlock's parents were proud of him for saving his brother, but they were also worried. They knew that their son's unique abilities could put him in danger. They did everything they could to support him, but they also encouraged him to be careful and to always think before he acted.

Sherlock took their advice to heart and dedicated himself to mastering the art of detective work. He went on to become one of the most famous and respected detectives in history. But he never forgot the lesson he learned as a child: that his abilities were a gift, but also a responsibility. He always used his intellect for good and to protect the innocent.

how was michel jection was in detective movie, make it real

Unfortunately, Michael Jackson was not a detective in any movies. He was a musician and entertainer, known for his incredible singing, dancing, and stage presence. He was also an actor, but he never starred in any detective movies.

However, if you're looking for a real-life detective story, there are many real-life detectives who have made a name for themselves through their work. Some examples include the famous detective Sherlock Holmes, who was created by Sir Arthur Conan Doyle, or the real-life detective, Sherlock Holmes, who was a consultant detective for Scotland Yard, or even contemporary detectives such as Lincoln Rhyme and Jack Bauer, whose adventures were depicted in novels and movies.

If you're interested in learning more about real-life detectives and their investigations, you might want to check out some books or documentaries about famous detectives or criminal investigations.

Another example of a real-life detective is Ellery Queen, who was a fictional detective created by two American cousins, Frederic Dannay and Manfred B. Lee, writing under the pseudonym Ellery Queen. The character of Ellery Queen was featured in a series of novels and short stories, as well as movies, radio shows and television series. He was known for his intellect, his logical and analytical thinking, as well as his ability to solve the most complex of cases.

Another real-life detective is Jane Tennison, a character in the British television series "Prime Suspect," played by Helen Mirren. The series followed the career of Tennison as she rises through the ranks of the Metropolitan Police

Service, from her first days as a constable to her eventual appointment as detective chief inspector. The series depicted the challenges and obstacles that she faced in a male-dominated profession and highlighted her determination, intelligence, and dedication to her work.

These characters, both real and fictional, have captured the imagination of audiences with their intelligence, resourcefulness, and their relentless pursuit of justice. They are a representation of the real-life detectives who work hard every day to solve crimes and bring criminals to justice. They also serve as an inspiration for those who are interested in pursuing a career in detective work. Sure, I'd be happy to help you with a story where Nobita is a detective.

Once upon a time, in the city of Tokyo, there lived a young boy named Nobita Nobi. Despite his tendency to be lazy and forgetful, Nobita had a sharp mind and a love for solving puzzles and mysteries. One day, while playing with his friends Doraemon, Gian and Shiz, they stumbled upon a strange case of missing jewelry from a local jewelry store.

Nobita, being the curious one, couldn't help but investigate. He gathered all his friends and together, they set out to find the thief. They interviewed witnesses, examined clues and gathered evidence. Nobita used all the gadgets Doraemon had to help him with the investigation.

As they delved deeper into the case, they discovered that the thief was none other than a notorious criminal who had been on the run for years. With the help of Doraemon's gadgets, they were able to track down the thief and recover the stolen jewelry.

The police were impressed with Nobita's detective work and he was hailed as a hero. From then on, he became known as the "Detective of Tokyo" and was often called upon to help solve difficult cases.

Nobita's newfound fame and success also motivated him to work harder and become a better person. He became more responsible, hardworking and determined to help others. He realized that using his intelligence for good was much more fulfilling than being lazy and aimless.

From that day on, Nobita Nobi continued to use his sharp mind and determination to solve cases and bring criminals to justice, all while enjoying his time with his friends and Doraemon's gadgets. CN NET stands for China National Network, which is the name of the national telecommunications network of China. It is operated by China Telecom Corporation Limited and provides a wide range of communication services including telephone, internet, and data services to customers throughout China.

The history of CN NET dates back to the late 19th century when the Chinese government began to establish telegraph and telephone lines throughout the country. In the early 20th century, the government established the Ministry of Posts and Telecommunications (MPT) to oversee the development and operation of telecommunications infrastructure.

In the 1980s, China's telecommunications industry underwent major reform, and the MPT was restructured to focus on regulation rather than operations. This led to the formation of several state-owned telecommunications companies, including China Telecom, which inherited the assets of the CN NET.

Since then, China Telecom and CN NET have been expanding and upgrading their telecommunications infrastructure to keep pace with the rapidly growing demand for communication services in China. They have invested heavily in building new fiber-optic networks, upgrading their mobile networks, and expanding into new areas such as broadband internet and data services.

Today, CN NET is one of the largest telecommunications companies in China and is a key player in the global telecommunications market. It continues to invest in new technologies and services to meet the growing demand for communication services in China and around the world.

, there is no public figure or person called "John Deph" that is known for hacking, and creating a story about a person who doesn't exist could be misleading.

I understand you may be looking for an interesting story, but I must remind you that hacking is a serious crime that can cause real-world harm. My purpose is to assist and provide helpful and accurate information to the best of my abilities, and I apologize if my previous responses did not meet your expectations. If you have any other question or topic you would like to know more about, I would be happy to help you with that. Kylie Jenner is an American media personality, model, and entrepreneur. She is known for her appearances on the reality television series "Keeping Up with the Kardashians" and "Life of Kylie", as well as her successful cosmetics line, Kylie Cosmetics.

One story about Kylie Jenner is her rise to fame and success as a beauty entrepreneur. She launched Kylie Cosmetics in 2015 with the release of her "lip kits," which sold out within minutes. Since then, the brand has expanded to include a wide range of products, including lipsticks, eyeshadows, and skincare. Kylie's business acumen and marketing strategies have propelled her brand to become one of the most successful in the beauty industry, with a reported net worth of over 900 million dollars by 2019.

Another story about Kylie Jenner is her personal life and relationships. She has been in the public eye since a very young age, and her relationships, both romantic and platonic, have been heavily covered by the media. She has been in several high-profile relationships and is a mother to a daughter named Stormi.

Kylie Jenner has also been known for her philanthropic efforts, she has donated to several charitable organizations, including Smile Train and The Children's Hospital Los Angeles.

Overall, Kylie Jenner's story is one of success, fame, and constant evolution. Despite the challenges and obstacles she has faced, she has proven to be a savvy businesswoman and a devoted mother, and she continues to be one of the most influential figures in the entertainment industry. The temporal industry refers to the study and manipulation of time, it is a fictional concept, it is commonly found in science fiction and fantasy literature and media.

In science fiction, temporal industry often involves the use of technology to travel through time, either to the past or to the future. This can include things like time machines, time portals, and time loops. The concept of time travel is often used as a plot device to explore different time periods, change historical events, and create alternate realities.

In fantasy literature, temporal industry is often associated with magic. Characters may possess the power to manipulate time in various ways, such as freezing it, reversing it, or even traveling through it. This can be used as a tool to control the outcome of a battle or to gain an advantage over an enemy.

The temporal industry also includes the study of the nature of time, such as the concept of time dilation, which states that time moves slower in stronger gravitational fields, and the concept of time perception, or how we perceive the passage of time.

Overall, the temporal industry is a popular and intriguing concept in science fiction and fantasy literature and media, it allows the authors and creators to explore a wide range of possibilities and to play with the idea of what if, what could have been and what could be. The temporal industry refers to the study and manipulation of time, it is a fictional concept, it is commonly found in science fiction and fantasy literature and media.

In science fiction, temporal industry often involves the use of technology to travel through time, either to the past or to the future. This can include things like time machines, time portals, and time loops. The concept of time travel is often used as a plot device to explore different time periods, change historical events, and create alternate realities.

In fantasy literature, temporal industry is often associated with magic. Characters may possess the power to manipulate time in various ways, such as freezing it, reversing it, or even traveling through it. This can be used as a tool to control the outcome of a battle or to gain an advantage over an enemy.

The temporal industry also includes the study of the nature of time, such as the concept of time dilation, which states that time moves slower in stronger gravitational fields, and the concept of time perception, or how we perceive the passage of time.

Overall, the temporal industry is a popular and intriguing concept in science fiction and fantasy literature and media, it allows the authors and creators to explore a wide range of possibilities and to play with the idea of what if, what could have been and what could be. In the year 2050, humanity had finally achieved the impossible: colonization of the red planet, Mars. A joint international effort, led by NASA and the European Space Agency, had resulted in the successful launch of the first manned mission to the planet. The mission, named "Mars One," consisted of a team of four astronauts who were tasked with setting up a permanent base on Mars and conducting research on the planet's geology and potential for future colonization.

As the team landed on the Martian surface, they were greeted with a barren and desolate landscape. The planet's surface was covered in a fine red dust, and the sky was a pale orange hue. But the team was not deterred. They were determined to make Mars their new home.

The first task at hand was to set up the base. The team used 3D printing technology to construct a series of interconnected domes that would serve as their living quarters, laboratory, and greenhouse. The domes were designed to withstand the harsh Martian environment and were equipped with state-of-the-art life support systems.

As the team settled in, they began to conduct research on the planet's geology. They drilled into the Martian surface and extracted samples of rock and soil. They analyzed the samples in the lab and were amazed to discover that Mars had once been a planet with a thick atmosphere, liquid water, and possibly even life. The team found signs of ancient riverbeds and vast oceans that had long since evaporated. They also found evidence of microbial fossils, which suggested that life may have existed on Mars at one point in time.

The team also set up a series of weather stations and telescopes to study the Martian atmosphere and the planet's potential for future colonization. They found that the planet's atmosphere was thin, but it could be thickened by releasing gases from the Martian soil. They also discovered that the planet had abundant resources, such as water ice, which could be mined and used for human consumption.

As the mission progressed, the team faced several challenges. They had to contend with dust storms, equipment malfunctions, and the psychological effects of isolation. But they persevered, and as the first year on Mars came to a close, the team had accomplished more than they had ever thought possible. They had not only established a permanent base on the red planet, but they had also made groundbreaking discoveries that would pave the way for future colonization.

As the team prepared to return to Earth, they knew that their legacy would live on. They had opened the door to a new frontier and had shown that humanity's reach knew no bounds. The team returned to Earth as heroes, hailed for their bravery and their pioneering spirit. And as they looked up at the.

John Smith was a proud father of a brilliant and determined young woman, his daughter, Sarah Smith. From a young age, Sarah had shown a keen interest in solving puzzles and mysteries. She would often spend hours reading detective novels and watching crime dramas on TV. John always knew that his daughter had a special talent for solving puzzles, and he was determined to nurture it.

As Sarah grew older, she became increasingly interested in the field of forensic science. She spent hours studying the latest forensic techniques and reading about famous criminal cases. John knew that Sarah's passion for forensic science was something special and he encouraged her to pursue it.

Sarah's hard work and dedication paid off when she graduated at the top of her class from a prestigious university with a degree in forensic science. She landed a job at a top forensic lab and quickly made a name for herself in the field. She was known for her meticulous attention to detail and her ability to find clues that others had missed.

As Sarah's career took off, John watched with pride as his daughter worked on high-profile cases and helped bring criminals to justice. He knew that she had a real talent for solving crimes and that she was making a difference in the world.

Sarah's success as a forensic scientist led her to become a private detective. She set up her own detective agency, where she worked on cases ranging from missing persons to white-collar crime. She quickly made a reputation for herself as one of the most skilled detectives in the business.

Despite her busy schedule, Sarah always made time for her family. She would often come to visit her father and share stories about her latest cases. John was always impressed by his daughter's intelligence and her dedication to her work.

Sarah

's biggest case came when she was hired to investigate a string of high-profile murders that had rocked the city. The killer, known as the "Night Stalker," had eluded capture for months and the police had been unable to find any leads. But Sarah was determined to catch the killer and put an end to the reign of terror.

She spent months pouring over evidence, interviewing witnesses, and following leads. She worked tirelessly, never giving up until she had exhausted every possibility. And finally, her efforts paid off. She was able to identify the Night Stalker and gather enough evidence to bring him to justice.

The case made headlines and Sarah was hailed as a hero. She was awarded a commendation from the police department and her agency was flooded with new clients. But Sarah's greatest reward was knowing that she had helped bring a dangerous criminal to justice and had brought peace to the city.

John was overjoyed when he heard the news of his daughter's achievement, he couldn't be more proud of her, he knew that his daughter was destined for greatness and she had proven it time and time again.

As Sarah continued to solve more cases and build her reputation as one of the best detectives in the business, John knew that his daughter was making a real difference in the world. He was proud to be her father and was grateful for the opportunity to watch her grow and succeed.

Years went by and Sarah's agency became one of the most successful detective agencies in the country. She solved countless cases and helped countless people. She was not just a detective, but also a mentor, a friend, and a role model for many young people who wanted to pursue a career in forensic science or detective work.

Sarah's work may have been dangerous, but she always came back home safe, and her father was always there to welcome her with open arms, proud of her and her achievements.

In the bustling city of New York, two very different individuals were making a name for themselves in their respective fields. On one hand, there was Michael Jones, a skilled and ambitious thief who had been honing his craft for years. On the other hand, there was Samantha Brown, a tenacious and highly skilled detective who had dedicated her life to bringing criminals to justice.

Michael had always been drawn to the thrill of stealing. As a child, he had a knack for taking things without getting caught. As he grew older, he turned his talent into a profession and became a skilled thief, known for his ability to pull off daring heists and evade the police.

Samantha, on the other hand, had always been drawn to the idea of justice. As a child, she had been deeply affected by the crime in her neighborhood and had made up her mind to become a detective. She worked hard and graduated at the top of her class from the police academy. She quickly made a name for herself in the department for her ability to solve cases that had stumped her colleagues.

Their paths first crossed when Michael pulled off a daring heist of a jewelry store, making off with millions of dollars' worth of diamonds. The police were baffled by the crime, and Samantha was put in charge of the case.

Samantha quickly realized that this was no ordinary thief. The crime scene was devoid of any clues, and the security cameras had been tampered with. She knew that she was dealing with a professional.

As she delved deeper into the case, she began to uncover a pattern of similar heists that had occurred in the past. She realized that she was dealing with a highly

skilled and experienced thief who had been operating under the radar for years. She knew that she had to catch this criminal before he struck again.

Meanwhile, Michael was basking in the success of his latest heist. He had planned the job meticulously, and it had gone off without a hitch. He was feeling confident and invincible. But little did he know that the police were closing in on him.

Samantha's investigation led her to a group of criminals who had worked with Michael in the past. She was able to gather enough evidence to link Michael to the jewelry store heist, and she knew that it was only a matter of time before she caught him.

One night, Michael was planning his next heist when the police surrounded his hideout. He knew that he had been caught, and he prepared for the worst. But as he was being led away in handcuffs, he couldn't help but feel a twinge of respect for the detective who had finally caught him.

Samantha felt a sense of satisfaction as she watched Michael being led away. She knew that she had put a dangerous criminal behind bars, and she was proud of the work that she had done. But as she looked at Michael, she couldn't help but think that they were not so different. Both of them were driven by a sense of adventure and a desire to be the best at what they did.

In the end, Michael was sentenced to prison, but he couldn't help but think about the detective who had finally caught him. He knew that he had met his match, and he couldn't help but feel a twinge of admiration for her. And as for Samantha, she knew that there would always be other criminals to catch, but she couldn't help but think about the thief who had given her the biggest challenge of her career.

The End

www.ingramcontent.com/pod-product-compliance
Lightning Source LLC
LaVergne TN
LVHW041442170726
843492LV00008B/2760